RuPaul Andre Charles:

Unveiling The Life And Biography Of RuPaul Andre Charles

Billie Davis

Table of Content

Introduction

There are individuals in the vast fabric of popular culture who go beyond simple celebrity to become something more—an enigmatic symbol. These exceptional people are distinguished by their deep influence on society as a whole, not just by their accomplishments or abilities. One such figure is RuPaul Andre Charles, better known by his first name, RuPaul. Exploring the worlds of entertainment, identity, and self-expression is necessary to grasp RuPaul's essence.

The world has been captivated by the phenomenon that is RuPaul, but the real RuPaul is a mystery that has only just begun to be told. Underneath the layers of ostentatious makeup, the tall wigs, and the glitzy outfits is a narrative of tenacity, change, and empowerment. This biography, "RuPaul Andre Charles: Unveiling The Life And Biography Of RuPaul Andre

Charles," aims to sift through these layers and dig into the life of the person who created the legend.

Establishing the Scene

We must first lay the foundation before we can fully comprehend RuPaul's rapid ascent and lasting influence. San Diego, California, a city on the edge of the cultural revolution, was the setting on November 17, 1960. A person who would question conventions and redefine beauty on a worldwide scale was born during the 1960s, a time of social turmoil and changing customs.

The birth of RuPaul was anything from typical. To combat institutional racism and discrimination, the civil rights movement was at its height at the time. The battle for the freedom to love and live without fear of retaliation was only starting to take shape at the time of the LGBTQ+ rights movement. RuPaul's journey started in the middle of this momentous time.

Early on, RuPaul displayed characteristics that would eventually come to characterize him: an unrepentant love of the limelight, an uncanny ability to draw attention, and an unwavering trust in himself. These early propensities paved the path for a future that not only broke through boundaries but also enabled others to do the same.

A young RuPaul had the ideal setting in San Diego to explore the worlds of identity and self-expression because of its varied and changing cultural scene. The seeds of originality were planted and the urge to stand out from the throng started to grow in this metropolis.

We will experience the difficulties RuPaul had in his early years, the crucial events that sparked his enthusiasm for the entertainment industry, and the unyielding resolve that drove him ahead as we go through the chapters of his life. We shall see the beginning of an icon, the birth of a movement, and the evolution of a person who would make a lasting impression on the globe.

We've set the scenario for the life of RuPaul Andre Charles and are getting ready to ride a wave of successes, setbacks, and disclosures. This biography will introduce you to the drag, music, media, and advocacy worlds while highlighting the varied genius of a great legend. Beyond the glitz and the celebrity, however, we will learn more about the real person who is as inspirational as the idol they have become.

As RuPaul, the mysterious legend, draws the curtains on his life, we cordially welcome you to enter a world of sparkling aspirations, unabashed candor, and the unwavering conviction that "you are born naked, and the rest is drag."

Chapter 1: Early Life

Born for Greatness

Greatness often has modest beginnings. RuPaul Andre Charles is not an exception to the conundrum that has persisted throughout history. RuPaul entered the earth on November 17, 1960, in San Diego, California, into a world full of promise, where the seeds of grandeur were sowed in the most humble of circumstances. Nobody could have predicted that this little boy would redefine beauty, defy social boundaries, and become a worldwide superstar with his alluring charm and limitless creativity.

RuPaul's Childhood: A Look Back

Early in childhood, RuPaul experienced both difficulties and bursts of inventiveness. Ernestine "Toni" and Irving Charles, who both had a significant impact on establishing his identity and worldview, were his parents when he was born. Young RuPaul found comfort and inspiration in the exciting world of television even if the Charles family had its share of financial difficulties.

RuPaul saw the constantly shifting cultural environment while growing up in the 1960s. The campaign for racial equality reverberated throughout the country during the height of the civil rights movement. A microcosm of these more significant social changes, San Diego's varied population became a strength. RuPaul's subsequent activism activity was shaped by his experience watching the civil rights movement.

RuPaul and his mother Toni Charles had a special relationship when they were young. She saw the remarkable spirit in her kid and nourished it with steadfast love. RuPaul gained the confidence that he could do everything he put his mind to from Toni, a creative and driven woman who was a force of nature herself.

Irving Charles, RuPaul's father, provided the framework and security that enabled RuPaul to pursue his huge dreams despite his less overt backing. The young RuPaul was profoundly influenced by his father's military experience and dedication to hard labor. His mother's inventiveness and his father's discipline combined to provide a powerful impact that would propel RuPaul's career forward.

'Finding a Passion

A spark of passion may light the way to greatness, and for RuPaul, that flame first appeared in his teens. He had a moth-like attraction to the entertainment industry as a young youngster. He used television as a window into the world outside of his immediate surroundings and as a canvas on which to express his aspirations.

Early fascinations of RuPaul with Hollywood stars, glitz, and the potential of metamorphosis would later be seen in his drag character. He would go on to honor the iconic performers who had caught his heart, all the while bringing his flair and charm to every performance.

RuPaul's chance discovery of a showing of the cult film "The Queen" at a nearby cinema was a turning point in his life. In the movie, competitors battled not only for crowns but also for the opportunity to show their real selves in the competitive and glamorous world of drag pageants. RuPaul was drawn inexorably into this culture of audacious self-expression.

RuPaul soon had an epiphany that would permanently alter the course of his life. Drag, he understood, was more than simply an artistic expression; it was also a potent tool for empowerment and self-discovery. Drag gave people like RuPaul and many others a way to accept their true selves at a time when being out homosexual was still frowned upon.

RuPaul started experimenting with drag, creating his identity and perfecting his performing abilities with the passion of a real visionary. The moment he took the stage as RuPaul for the first time, a power that would enthrall audiences everywhere was unleashed. He was unaware that this was just the start of an unbelievable trip.

Chapter 2: The Rise of RuPaul

The Path to Stardom

Every celebrity has a "moment of inception," a time when their brilliance first emerges. In the thriving and diverse environment of New York City in the early 1980s, RuPaul Andre Charles experienced that time. It was a city renowned for its variety, inventiveness, and promise of limitless opportunities—the ideal setting for RuPaul's rise to fame.

A mix of tenacity, ingenuity, and an unwavering faith in his own abilities defined RuPaul's path from a young child with ambitions to a budding drag phenomenon. He would discover the blank canvas he needed to create his own tale in the center of the Big Apple.

RuPaul's Drag: The Beginning

A wave of inspiration hit RuPaul as soon as he set foot on the streets of New York City. His development into the recognizable figure we know today took place against the background of the city's burgeoning underground club scene. RuPaul's drag character started to take form at these seedy, cutting-edge nightclubs.

Early drag performances by RuPaul defied conventional ideas of gender and attractiveness by embracing the outspoken androgyny of the time. He wasn't simply a performance; he was a message, the living proof that one might find beauty in one's own expression. This unafraid attitude to drag was a break from the norm, and it put RuPaul on the path to fame.

Beyond his performances, RuPaul had a significant impact. In extending the possibilities of drag, he was a pioneer. RuPaul was already embracing gender fluidity at a time when the rest of the world was only beginning to understand it.

He delivered a straightforward message: Be who you are, without apology or concession.

Early Career Challenges

Although RuPaul's ability and charm were evident, his ascent to prominence wasn't without its share of difficulties. RuPaul was not an exception to the rule that success is often accompanied by setbacks and times of uncertainty.

RuPaul struggled financially at the beginning of his career and was unsure of where his next meal would come from. While pursuing his love for drag, he did odd jobs, including a short period as a used car dealer. However, these challenges only strengthened his will to prevail.

RuPaul's encounter with the renowned musician and producer Larry Tee was one of his career's turning points. The result of their collaboration was the number-one single "Supermodel (You Better Work)," which propelled RuPaul into the mainstream music business. The upbeat song went on to become an anthem of empowerment and self-assurance, and RuPaul's career turned around as a result of its popularity.

RuPaul's popularity increased as "Supermodel" ruled the radio and the charts. He established himself as a regular on television, making appearances on talk programs and in music videos. He even got his own talk show, "The RuPaul Show." RuPaul had evolved into more than simply a drag performer; he was now a household name.

Chapter 3: The Drag Revolution

Changing the Landscape

A cultural tidal wave known as the "Drag Revolution" completely altered the entertainment, fashion, and self-expression industries. It honored the art of drag in ways that were previously unthinkable, it defied standards, and it broke down boundaries. This chapter explores the seismic upheavals that occurred, the development of a drag queen with a cause, and the classic song that would eventually become the movement's anthem.

Drag was mostly associated with the underground environment before the Drag Revolution. There, artists and performers could express their creativity and gender identity in ways that were often disapproved of or ostracized by society. It was a subculture that was concealed from the public. Drag kings and queens have pushed the envelope, disproved prejudices, and explored the wide range of gender and self-identity. But it was a world that lived outside of popular society, in smoky pubs and clubs, hidden from prying eyes.

All of this started to alter in the late 20th century when several occasions and cultural transformations came together to provide the ideal storm for the Drag Revolution. The growing agitation for LGBTQ+ rights was one of the major drivers. The Stonewall riots in 1969, which are often seen as the beginning of the contemporary LGBTQ+ rights movement, constituted a watershed. Drag queens, such as Marsha P. Johnson and Sylvia Rivera, were key participants in those historic demonstrations against discrimination and police brutality. Their advocacy paved the path for the LGBTQ+ community's increased exposure and acceptance.

In parallel, the entertainment industry was going through a change of its own. With the emergence of reality television, there was a new venue for showing skill, quirkiness, and individualism. The pioneering reality competition program RuPaul's Drag Race, which debuted in 2009, highlighted drag queens from all around the United States. It was not simply popular; it was also a part of popular culture. Millions of spectators were exposed to the art of drag as a result of the program, which provided drag queens with a national platform to showcase their abilities and personalities.

RuPaul's Drag Race's popularity served as a symbol of a more general societal change toward inclusiveness and the celebration of diversity. It wasn't only about drag as a kind of entertainment; it was also about honoring the talent and bravery of the queens who had, for so long, been kept in the background. The significance of self-expression, self-love, and the strength of accepting one's personality were all highlighted throughout the program.

Drag started to ingratiate itself into popular culture as the program gained more and more viewers. The media began to feature drag queens and their well-known catchphrases. The fashion industry took note, and well-known designers began working with drag queens and using them in their advertising campaigns. Drag was abruptly removed from the shadows and thrust into the limelight, altering the face of entertainment, fashion, and self-expression.

The drag queen with a purpose

RuPaul Charles stood out as a change- and empowerment-beacon in the middle of this movement. In addition to being the face of drag, RuPaul—a skilled drag performer with a background in music and acting—became a key figure in the LGBTQ+ rights movement. He wasn't simply a drag artist; he was an artist on a mission.

The purpose of RuPaul's life was to inspire love, self-acceptance, and empowerment. He mentored and inspired budding drag queens by using his platform on RuPaul's Drag Race. His tagline, "If you can't love yourself, how in the hell are you gonna love somebody else?" became a mantra for accepting and loving oneself. Many people have been motivated to embrace their genuine selves by RuPaul's unabashed confidence and honesty, which connected with both spectators and competitors.

RuPaul's influence, however, went beyond television. He made use of his prominence to promote acceptance and rights for LGBTQ+ people. Regardless of society's conventions or expectations, he exhorted individuals to be their true selves. Drag demonstrated that it was more than simply an art form and could be a potent force for social change. RuPaul's daring self-expression pushed the limits of gender and identity.

RuPaul's capacity to shatter gender norms and broaden the notion of beauty was one of his most important contributions to the drag movement.

RuPaul promoted variety and exhorted queens to be true to themselves in a culture that sometimes maintained limited ideals of beauty. To express the ferocious and self-assured character that drag queens might convey, he created the word "glamazon," which combines splendor with Amazonian strength.

Contestants on RuPaul's Drag Race were urged to emphasize their uniqueness, and the program honored queens of different ages, genders, and ethnic origins. A wider acceptance of all body shapes, races, and gender identities resulted from this strategy's challenge to the fashion and beauty sectors to become more inclusive and varied.

RuPaul also utilized music to spread his optimistic and self-empowerment message. "Supermodel (You Better Work)," one of his most well-known songs, ended up serving as the Drag Revolution's anthem. The 1992 song's infectious melody and uplifting lyrics perfectly encapsulated the spirit of drag culture and its self-assurance message. Anyone aiming to be their best and most genuine selves will find inspiration in the chorus "You better work," which has become a catchphrase.

The "Supermodel (You Better Work)" music video established RuPaul's influence on the entertainment business. In the film, a varied group of drag queens displayed their originality and sassy style. The assertion that drag queens were not just creatives but also trendsetters who were defying convention and reinventing beauty ideals was audacious.

"Supermodel (You Better Work)"

A cultural phenomenon that embodied the spirit of the Drag Revolution, "Supermodel (You Better Work)" was more than simply a song. The song, which served as the first single for RuPaul's debut album, "Supermodel of the World," became viral right away after its release. It became a hit right away because of the song's catchy lyrics, snappy dance tempo, and captivating delivery by RuPaul.

The straightforward but impactful words of "Supermodel (You Better Work)" were excellent. They promoted self-expression, self-assurance, and the notion that everybody could be a supermodel in their own right. The song promoted the notion that beauty comes in all shapes and sizes and that real beauty is about accepting one's individuality.

The song "Supermodel (You Better Work)" has an equally well-known music video. RuPaul was shown strutting her thing on a fashion runway while being accompanied by a varied array of drag queens in the video, which was directed by Randy Barbato and Fenton Bailey. A feast of lavish clothing, furious stances, and unabashed self-expression filled the film. It made it quite evident that drag queens were not just fashion stars and trendsetters, but also entertainers.

"Supermodel (You Better Work)" has an effect beyond the drag and music industries. It became a song of empowerment and confidence in oneself. The song's message was welcomed by people from all walks of life, not only LGBTQ+ people. Its slogan, "You better work," became a well-known maxim for everyone attempting to be their best and most genuine selves.

RuPaul became the mainstream thanks in part to the song's popularity. It was the start of a fruitful music career for him, during which he would put out multiple albums and songs. With its message of optimism, acceptance, and celebration, RuPaul's music became the soundtrack for the LGBTQ+ community and its supporters.

The fashion industry was greatly impacted by "Supermodel (You Better Work)" as well. The song's lyrics and music video praised the notion that fashion was a means of self-expression and that there were no restrictions on individuality in terms of personal style. This message struck a chord with fashion fans, models, and designers, leading to a greater focus on variety and originality in the fashion industry.

Beyond the music video, RuPaul had an impact on fashion. He became a favorite front-row spot at fashion shows and an inspiration for well-known designers. With his presence, the business was pushed to be more diverse and to acknowledge the diversity of beauty. Fashion designers were motivated to break boundaries and celebrate diversity on the catwalk by RuPaul's outspoken and unabashed sense of style.

"Supermodel (You Better Work)" influences the LGBTQ+ community, which is one of its lasting legacies. LGBTQ+ people, who often experienced prejudice and had a hard time accepting themselves, adopted the song as their anthem. A feeling of pride and belonging was given by its message of empowerment and self-assurance. The song's creator, RuPaul, became a representation of resiliency and optimism for many.

The song was played often during LGBTQ+ pride celebrations to energize the audience and foster a feeling of cohesion and self-assurance, extending its impact on those communities. During pride parades and festivals, it was not unusual to see drag queens and LGBTQ+ people dancing and expressing their identities to the catchy rhythm of "Supermodel (You Better Work)".

Another song that helped dispel myths and assumptions about drag queens was "Supermodel (You Better Work)". Drag was often misunderstood and inaccurately portrayed in the media before the Drag Revolution. Drag queens were often shown as caricatures or as objects of mockery. With its message of fiery confidence and self-expression, RuPaul's song and music video sent a distinct message. It contributed to redefining how society saw drag queens and opened the door to more acceptance and comprehension.

"Supermodel (You Better Work)" had an effect outside of the United States. Despite linguistic and cultural obstacles, it found resonance with individuals all across the globe. Drag queens from many nations welcomed the song and its message, including it into their shows, and utilizing it to propagate the Drag Revolution's message of self-acceptance and empowerment.

After the success of "Supermodel (You Better Work)," RuPaul remained a major influence in the drag and LGBTQ+ communities. He promoted acceptance, mentored emerging drag queens, and spoke out for LGBTQ+ rights using his platform. A new generation of drag artists and viewers were motivated by RuPaul's Drag Race, which saw continuing growth in popularity.

Other drag queens who wanted to work in music, acting, or fashion were able to do so thanks to the popularity of "Supermodel (You Better Work)". It proved that drag was not a constraint but rather a platform for boundless creativity and self-expression. Drag queens that found success via the program, like Trixie Mattel, Adore Delano, and Alaska Thunderfuck, went on to create their songs and leave their imprint in the entertainment business.

Drag developed and gained widespread acceptability, becoming a potent force for social change. Drag queens have utilized their fame and platforms to promote LGBTQ+ rights, gender equality, and acceptance of all people, regardless of their sexual orientation or gender identity. A more welcoming and inclusive society has resulted from the Drag Revolution, which has also altered the entertainment and fashion industries.

Drag culture has a significant effect on society as seen by the song's continuing influence on the music, fashion, and LGBTQ+ rights industries. It serves as a reminder that expressing one's actual self, dismantling stereotypes, and questioning social conventions are effective means of bringing about constructive change.

With "Supermodel (You Better Work)" as its theme song, the drag revolution has persisted in motivating people all over the globe to embrace their unique personalities and the virtues of variety.

Chapter 4: Becoming a Household Name

The 90s: A Decade of Influence

The advent of drag as a popular phenomenon and the ascent of RuPaul to the status of an iconic figure made the 1990s a pivotal decade for drag culture. In this chapter, we discuss the cultural climate of the 1990s and how it paved the way for drag to become well-known.

A lot of cultural change and turmoil occurred throughout the 1990s. It came after the turbulent 1980s, which saw the rise of the LGBTQ+ rights movement, the AIDS crisis, and a rising need for visibility and acceptance. The LGBTQ+ community and its supporters persisted in their quest for recognition in popular culture and media as the decade progressed.

The 1990 release of Madonna's "Vogue" was one of the crucial turning points that paved the way for the emergence of drag. The song and its music video honored the art of voguing, a dance form with origins in the LGBTQ+ community's ballroom culture, notably among Black and Latinx LGBTQ+ people. Drag and queer performance became more prominent as a result of Madonna's introduction of voguing into popular culture.

In addition to introducing millions of people to the world of drag, "Vogue" also showed how powerful LGBTQ+ creativity and self-expression can be. Famous Hollywood actors and supermodels were alluded to in the song's lyrics, connecting them to the glitzy and sassy world of drag. It was a statement that drag was attractive, creative, and worthy of celebration and had something to give outside the underground environment.

Drag began to become more visible in movies and television as the 1990s went on. films like

"To Wong Foo, Thanks for Everything! " and "The Adventures of Priscilla, Queen of the Desert" (1994) are examples of this. Julie Newmar" (1995) challenged prejudices and humanized the drag experience by portraying drag queens as vibrant and endearing people. Drag became more approachable and less stigmatized thanks to the films that made it more widely known.

Drag was prominently shown thanks to a large part of television programs. Viewers could see the amazing creativity and internal changes that drag queens and kings through on episodes of "The Jenny Jones Show" and "The Ricki Lake Show," which regularly aired segments centered on drag transformations. Drag queens were given a platform by these programs to showcase their skills and share their narratives with a wide audience.

Drag enters the mainstream

When "RuPaul's Drag Race" debuted in 2009, it was the true turning point for drag's acceptability by the general public. Even though the first season of this reality competition series didn't premiere until the twenty-first century, its influence on drag and LGBTQ+ culture can be dated back to the late 1990s, when RuPaul was already a well-known figure in the drag community.

Drag was introduced into millions of viewers' living rooms by RuPaul, who had previously established himself as a drag performer, singer, and actor. "RuPaul's Drag Race" broke new ground by showcasing the talent, originality, and ferocious competition of drag queens from all around the United States. To become "America's Next Drag Superstar," contestants participated in a variety of tasks, including acting tests and fashion runways.

The style of the event not only showcased the tremendous abilities of drag performers but also gave them a stage on which to discuss their hardships, victories, and personal tales. The contestants often discussed the significance of drag in their lives, their experiences with prejudice, and coming out. Audiences found this blend of fun and real stories to be compelling, and it also helped to humanize the drag experience.

"RuPaul's Drag Race" exposed fans to a wide range of drag queens, each with their distinct style and history. This variety dispelled many misconceptions about drag and proved that there is no one "correct" way to do drag. It promoted inclusiveness and acceptance by honoring drag queens of various sexes, ethnicities, and socioeconomic status.

The popularity of "RuPaul's Drag Race" contributed to the popularization of drag. The program developed a devoted audience in addition to receiving favorable reviews and winning various accolades. With allusions to the program and its catchphrases in popular culture, fashion, and social media, it helped drag become more widely accepted.

One of the distinguishing characteristics of "RuPaul's Drag Race" was RuPaul's function as a mentor and advisor to the competitors. He taught me priceless lessons in self-empowerment and self-acceptance through his charm, confidence, and knowledge. Fans adopted RuPaul's catchphrases as mantras of self-love and resiliency, such as "Sashay away" and "If you can't love yourself, how in the hell are you gonna love somebody else"

Drag queens and their lavish runway outfits served as a source of inspiration for designers and fashion fans in the fashion industry as a result of the show's influence. Bold and eccentric fashion trends are becoming more widely accepted because of the "Drag Race effect". Drag queens like Violet Chachki, Aquaria, and Shea Couleé displayed their distinct fashion senses on the program, defying societal expectations of beauty and promoting individual expression via dress.

As "RuPaul's Drag Race" gained more and more acclaim, a franchise was created that included RuPaul's DragCon and foreign versions of the program as well as spin-offs. Fans have a place to meet their favorite queens, enjoy drag culture, and engage in unrestricted self-expression at DragCon. It came to symbolize the wide-ranging influence of drag on popular culture.

Influence of RuPaul on LGBTQ+ Culture

Beyond drag, RuPaul had a significant impact on LGBTQ+ culture. He rose to prominence in the struggle for acceptance and rights for LGBTQ+ people. He powerfully demonstrated that LGBTQ+ people may accomplish their goals and be authentically themselves via his career and exposure as a drag queen.

RuPaul utilized his position to campaign for LGBTQ+ rights, raising concerns about things like prejudice and marriage equality. Despite the challenges they encountered, he underlined the value of self-acceptance and exhorted LGBTQ+ people to embrace who they are. Many members of the LGBTQ+ community look up to RuPaul because of his tenacity and genuineness.

Along with his efforts, LGBTQ+ people continued to find inspiration and pride in RuPaul's songs. Songs like "Cover Girl (Put the Bass in Your Walk)" and "Supermodel (You Better Work)" were anthems that praised self-expression and confidence. To encourage individuals to love and accept themselves for who they were, they were often played at LGBTQ+ pride events and celebrations.

When RuPaul became the first drag queen to get a star on the Hollywood Walk of Fame in 2018, his notoriety and influence on LGBTQ+ culture were further cemented. This distinction represented a major change in society's recognition of drag as a valid and respected art form in addition to recognizing his achievements to the entertainment industry.

values and culture.

The progression of LGBTQ+ acceptance and representation may be seen in RuPaul's rise from a drag performer to a cultural superstar. His popularity upended conventional conventions and expectations, demonstrating that drag queens could be more than simply showgirls and inspirations for a multicultural and accepting society.

Drag gained popularity because of programs like "RuPaul's Drag Race," which opened the path for a more widespread acceptance of LGBTQ+ people. Drag kings and queens often utilized their platform to talk about personal issues like coming out, prejudice, and difficulties they had. This transparency made LGBTQ+ topics more relatable and encouraged people to empathize with and understand the concerns.

"RuPaul's Drag Race" was able to foster a feeling of solidarity and community, which is one of its most important contributions to LGBTQ+ culture. The candidates of the program often formed strong ties with one another, highlighting the value of chosen family and support for one another. This message connected with LGBTQ+ people who may have experienced rejection from their biological families, giving them a feeling of acceptance and belonging within the drag community.

The success of the program also encouraged a new generation of LGBTQ+ young people to accept their identities and find strength in their differences. The varied cast of queens and kings served as mirrors for many spectators, who realized they could be proud of who they were. As a result of this empowerment, LGBTQ+ people now feel more at ease being themselves in a more tolerant and inclusive society.

Beyond the confines of television, RuPaul had a significant influence on LGBTQ+ culture. He advocated for LGBTQ+ concerns and raised awareness of them via the use of his platform. His exposure as a drag queen and his courageous activism helped combat prejudice and discrimination as well as de-stigmatize LGBTQ+ concerns.

In the struggle for marriage equality, RuPaul's support was extremely important. He took advantage of his position to advocate for same-sex unions and urged others to follow suit. His success as a drag performer who had discovered true love and happiness with his spouse challenged prejudices against LGBTQ+ partnerships and helped change the public's perception of marriage equality.

Along with supporting LGBTQ+ rights, RuPaul emphasized the significance of self-acceptance and self-love. Many LGBTQ+ people who were dealing with their sense of self-worth and self-identity adopted his tagline, "If you can't love yourself, how in the hell are you gonna love somebody else?" as a motto. Those who have experienced prejudice or internalized homophobia responded strongly to RuPaul's message of self-empowerment.

In his work outside of "RuPaul's Drag Race," RuPaul has affected LGBTQ+ culture. To disseminate his message of self-assurance, sincerity, and resiliency, he continued to record music, publish books, and appear in public. His autobiography, "Lettin' It All Hang Out," gave readers a real-life glimpse into his challenges and life path, offering comfort and encouragement to those who could identify with his experiences.

RuPaul's impact has spread to the fashion industry. For designers and fashion fans, his flamboyant and avant-garde style served as an inspiration. RuPaul and other drag queens defied conventional beauty standards and opened the path for a broader acceptance of distinctive and outlandish fashion choices with their bold commitment to self-expression. RuPaul's influence on the fashion industry extended beyond apparel to include appreciating uniqueness and promoting diversity.

RuPaul has continued to influence mainstream entertainment and LGBTQ+ culture in recent years. International editions of "RuPaul's Drag Race" have been added, promoting drag culture to a wider audience and encouraging a feeling of community and appreciation of variety. Drag has firmly cemented its position in popular society because of the success of the show's winners in a variety of spheres, including music, acting, activism, and business.

RuPaul's transformation from a drag queen to a cultural icon and campaigner is an example of the wider advancements in LGBTQ+ acceptance and visibility. He has created a lasting legacy that continues to empower LGBTQ+ people and encourage a more tolerant and inclusive society because of his ability to question cultural standards and promote self-acceptance. Drag has become a household brand because of RuPaul's efforts, yet it has also evolved into a force for good and a celebration of diversity.

Chapter 5: RuPaul's Drag Race

The Birth of a Cultural Phenomenon

"RuPaul's Drag Race" has had a profound cultural impact on drag culture, LGBTQ+ representation, and the world of entertainment. It is more than simply a reality competition program. The show's beginnings, development, and significant influence on drag culture and society at large are all covered in this chapter.

The idea for "RuPaul's Drag Race" sprang from RuPaul's desire to popularize drag and provide drag queens with a stage on which to display their skills and creativity. Even though RuPaul was already successful as a drag queen, singer, and actor, he wanted to provide a platform where other queens could shine and tell their tales.

In 2009, RuPaul served as the host and chief judge of the program, which premiered on the Logo network. From the start, "RuPaul's Drag Race" distinguished itself from other reality competition programs. It mixed aspects of competition, innovation, and personal narrative to give viewers a distinctive and captivating experience.

One of the most important developments in the program was the addition of tasks that evaluated many facets of a queen's aptitude and abilities. Contestants had to show off their talent at lip-syncing, humor, acting, and fashion. The wide variety of difficulties not only demonstrated the adaptability of drag queens but also enabled spectators to grasp the breadth of their abilities.

The focus placed on the transformation process in "RuPaul's Drag Race" was another key feature. In a mini-challenge that was part of every show, the queens had a short window of time to come up with a distinctive outfit or complete a job. This demonstrated the inventiveness, ingenuity, and fast thinking needed in the drag community. It also gave spectators an understanding of the preparations that went into a queen's look and performance.

But the runway portion was the show's centerpiece. Here, queens showcased their expertly constructed outfits, which were often motivated by a theme or challenge. The runway served as a venue for narrative, creativity, and self-expression. It gave queens the chance to delve into many facets of their identities, such as their personal histories and cultural backgrounds.

Lip-syncing is a fundamental component of drag performances, and "RuPaul's Drag Race" introduced audiences to the technique. The show's infamous lip-sync bouts became one of its defining moments, displaying the queens' capacity to convey the passion of the song to the audience while captivating them. These lip-sync performances often showed the intensity of a queen's devotion and willpower to continue competing.

As the program went on, it became evident that "RuPaul's Drag Race" was about the queens' individual experiences, not simply drag acts. The contestants often discussed the difficulties they had as LGBTQ+ people, including coming out and encountering prejudice. These touching and exposed moments forged a strong connection between the queens and the audience, promoting compassion and understanding.

A look into Drag Race's production process

Behind the scenes, "RuPaul's Drag Race" was a labor of love, inventiveness, and hard work, despite the polished and entertaining appearance it gave on TV. The show's production staff, which included producers, costume designers, makeup artists, and directors, was essential in realizing the idea.

The show's commitment to authenticity was one of the main factors in its popularity. The material of "RuPaul's Drag Race" was neither scripted nor staged, in contrast to many reality series. The spectators felt a feeling of justice and honesty since the tasks, exchanges, and eliminations were all genuine.

The show's crew gave the queens assistance and mentoring behind the scenes. They had access to makeup artists and stylists who helped them refine their appearances and take on the gorgeous and fearless personalities we saw on film. The queens worked together with makeup artists, hairstylists, and costume designers to develop their drag personalities throughout the transformation process.

The show's creators and therapists also supported the queens' emotional development. The ability for contestants to discuss their sentiments and experiences gave them a secure place to vent their opinions and frailties. By demonstrating that the opulent identities were only a front for real people with genuine experiences, this part of the program served to humanize the queens.

RuPaul was one of the judges, and they all contributed a ton of knowledge and experience to the competition. They offered advice and helpful criticism in addition to rating the queens' performances in their reviews. The judges were crucial in assisting the queens in developing as artists and performers.

The intensity of the competition was one of "RuPaul's Drag Race"'s most difficult parts for the queens. The candidates were put through their physical and emotional paces by the show's strict shooting schedule, long hours, and difficult obstacles. They needed to have resiliency, flexibility, and self-assurance.

Behind the scenes, the queens' tenacity and hard ethic were often on full show. They put in endless hours improving their appearances, practicing their acts, and helping one another.

The friendship among the competitors was evidence of the feeling of community that existed in the drag culture.

The show's competitive element, in which queens were subject to eviction each week, generated drama and intrigue that captivated viewers. Knowing that their fellow contestants were facing the same difficulties and pressures, also meant that queens often formed deep relationships with one another.

"RuPaul's Drag Race" stressed the value of sisterhood and solidarity among the queens despite its competitive character. There were many instances of empathy and connection as a result of contestants sharing their hardships and tales. Many queens developed enduring relationships and worked together with their fellow contestants after the event, demonstrating how this feeling of community persisted.

Drag Culture's Effect on The Show

"RuPaul's Drag Race" has had a significant and pervasive influence on drag culture, both within the LGBTQ+ community and in general society. The show's impact is evident in several significant areas, such as increased exposure, better acceptance, and the elevation of drag as an art form.

First and foremost, "RuPaul's Drag Race" made drag more widely accepted. It dispelled prejudices and exposed millions of viewers to the artistry, originality, and brilliance of drag queens. There is no one "right" way to perform drag, as shown by the show's eclectic roster of queens, who displayed a variety of styles and backgrounds.

It is impossible to overestimate the show's effect on LGBTQ+ representation. It gave LGBTQ+ youngsters role models and heroes to look up to, demonstrating to them that it was possible to be proud of who they were and to follow their ambitions. The queens on the program often recounted their personal stories, including their experiences with prejudice and coming out, giving viewers who experienced the same difficulties encouragement and hope.

"RuPaul's Drag Race" made a significant contribution to the societal acceptance of LGBTQ+ people. It emphasized drag queens' resiliency and innovation while humanizing their situations. The program helped viewers who may not have had much exposure to LGBTQ+ issues develop a greater understanding and empathy.

Drag queens and their lavish runway outfits served as a source of inspiration for designers and fashion fans in the fashion industry as a result of the show's influence. Drag queens like RuPaul disrupted conventional notions of beauty and promoted individuality via clothes because of their bold self-expression.

"RuPaul's Drag Race" has affected the entertainment business as well as LGBTQ+ culture and acceptance. Drag queens now have more employment options than ever before, including acting, modeling, and the performing arts. Numerous participants from the program have produced their songs, had cameo appearances in motion pictures and television shows, and even adorned the pages of fashion publications. Drag's position in popular culture has been further cemented by its extension into mainstream entertainment.

The show's effects on the entertainment market are notably noticeable in the music sector. The "RuPaul's Drag Race" contestants who went on to make popular music albums and singles include many queens. Numerous songs performed by drag queens on the program have become dance floor anthems at LGBTQ+ gatherings and clubs.

An outstanding example is Season 5 "RuPaul's Drag Race" competitor Alaska Thunderfuck.

Since then, Alaska has published several albums and songs, and her work has gained not just acclaim within the LGBTQ+ community but also across the larger music business. The possibility for drag queens to succeed in the music business is shown by her success as a recording artist.

A forum for queens to voice their activism and promote social change has also been made available by the event. Many queens have taken use of their increased prominence to spread the word about crucial problems including mental health, HIV/AIDS awareness, and the rights of LGBTQ+ people. These queens have influenced change in their communities and contributed significantly to social justice problems via their work as advocates.

The influence "RuPaul's Drag Race" has on drag as an art form is among its most lasting legacies. Drag has now become a revered and acclaimed art form thanks to the television program. By defying preconceptions and securing a space for drag on famous stages and in art galleries, it has shown the enormous ability, ingenuity, and passion that drag queens bring to their trade.

In terms of diversity and representation, "RuPaul's Drag Race" has also had an impact on drag culture. The program has drawn criticism for certain areas of diversity, such as the portrayal of transgender and non-binary queens, but it has also contributed to conversations about these topics within the drag community. Within the drag community, there have been significant changes and raised awareness as a result of the discourse around diversity and representation.

The influence of the event has also been felt on a global scale. "RuPaul's Drag Race" served as the model for other overseas spinoffs, including "RuPaul's Drag Race UK," "RuPaul's Drag Race Canada," and "RuPaul's Drag Race Down Under." The appeal of drag culture has been furthered by these spin-offs, which have exposed viewers from all over the globe to regional drag scenes and queens.

"RuPaul's Drag Race" has also given rise to a successful conference called RuPaul's DragCon. Fans may meet their favorite queens at the convention, take in discussions, and celebrate all facets of drag culture. RuPaul's DragCon has developed into an annual occasion in several places, bringing together fans of drag from all backgrounds to savor the beauty and innovation of drag.

Last but not least, Chapter 5 of "RuPaul's Drag Race" examines the genesis of a phenomenon that has profoundly influenced entertainment, drag culture, and LGBTQ+ visibility. Drag has been transformed from an unheralded subculture to a revered art form because of the show's distinctive blend of competition, inventiveness, and personal narrative, which has won over fans' hearts.

"RuPaul's Drag Race" has improved the exposure and acceptability of drag queens while also giving them the chance to pursue professions in a variety of industries, including activism, music, and acting. The show's impact goes beyond the realm of entertainment, igniting discussions about diversity and representation both within the drag community and the larger LGBTQ+ movement.

"RuPaul's Drag Race" has helped LGBTQ+ people and their supporters feel a feeling of camaraderie, acceptance, and empowerment. The program has inspired viewers to accept their real selves by showcasing the queens' individual experiences. A testimony to the strength of sincerity, imagination, and self-expression is the show's influence on drag culture and society in general.

Chapter 6: Beyond Drag Race

RuPaul's Multi-Faceted Career

Although "RuPaul's Drag Race" continues to be one of RuPaul Charles' most recognizable and impactful contributions to popular culture, his work goes well beyond the confines of the reality competition program. In this chapter, we examine the many facets of RuPaul's career, from his successes in music and television to his activism and charitable endeavors.

RuPaul's ascent to fame was a lengthy and laborious one that was distinguished by tenacity and a firm trust in himself. RuPaul Andre Charles was raised in a working-class home and was born on November 17, 1960, in San Diego, California. RuPaul showed a talent for performing as well as a love of glitz and style from an early age. The basis for his future career in entertainment was built by his early interests in theater and music.

As a musician, RuPaul made one of his first forays into the entertainment business. In 1993, "Supermodel of the World," his first album, was made available. The album's number-one song, "Supermodel (You Better Work)," launched him to prominence throughout the world. RuPaul's position in music history was cemented by the song's popularity, which also established him as a household celebrity.

Several further albums, such as "Foxy Lady" (1996), "Ho Ho Ho" (1997), and "Red Hot" (2004), were released after "Supermodel of the World." Dance-pop to R&B were among the genres represented in RuPaul's music, which also included catchy, empowering, and often goofy songs. His place as a pop culture hero was further solidified by the bright graphics and unique clothing seen in his music videos.

RuPaul pursued acting and television presenting in addition to his music career. He had many film and television appearances, including "The Brady Bunch Movie" (1995), "To Wong Foo, Thanks for Everything! Julie Newmar," and "But I'm a Cheerleader," both from 1999. Through these roles, RuPaul was able to demonstrate his charm, comedy, and range as a performer.

With his talk program, "The RuPaul Show," which ran from 1996 to 1998, RuPaul first entered the world of television hosting. The program included conversations on many subjects, music performances, and celebrity interviews—all of which were imbued with RuPaul's endearing charm and humor. For its time, "The RuPaul Show" was revolutionary because it gave LGBTQ+ voices and causes a forum.

RuPaul's position as a television star, however, was cemented with "RuPaul's Drag Race". The reality competition program, which debuted in 2009 and has since grown in popularity, is still one of the most watched and adored reality shows. In his capacity as the show's host and chief judge, RuPaul was able to provide advice, comedy, and guidance to budding drag queens and performers.

RuPaul has an impact on the fashion sector in addition to his work in music and television. He became a fashion icon for well-known designers because of his audacious and unapologetic look, which was distinguished by lavish outfits, ornate wigs, and immaculate makeup. Inspiring designers to embrace diversity and self-expression on the catwalk, he often frequented the front rows of fashion events.

RuPaul's message as well as his style affected the fashion industry. He promoted self-acceptance and questioned gender and attractiveness expectations in society. RuPaul's catchphrase, "We're all born naked, and the rest is drag," stressed that everyone projects an image to the outside world, whether or not they are in drag.

Music, TV, Film

His reputation as a multi-talented performer has been cemented by RuPaul's successes in music, television, and cinema. Particularly his music career has had an everlasting impression on the mainstream cultural landscape. The song "Supermodel (You Better Work)" from his first album, "Supermodel of the World," has become a symbol of empowerment and self-assurance.

Millions of people were enthralled by the song's famous music video and catchy tempo, as well as its captivating lyrics. Regardless of their gender identity or sexual orientation, listeners were moved by RuPaul's message of self-acceptance and embracing one's individuality. A significant moment in LGBTQ+ and popular culture history, "Supermodel (You Better Work)" broke through barriers and questioned social conventions.

RuPaul kept putting out songs throughout his career, experimenting with different musical styles and subjects. His albums often mixed dance-pop songs with melancholy ballads, demonstrating both his vocal range and his flexibility as an artist. While his songs may not have always been the most popular, they always conveyed a message of self-love and sincerity.

RuPaul has pursued acting in addition to his singing career, both on the big screen and on television. He displayed his comic skill and enduring presence in "The Brady Bunch Movie" as Mrs. Cummings, the guidance counselor. However, his performance opposite Wesley Snipes and Patrick Swayze in "To Wong Foo, Thanks for Everything! Julie Newmar" was what cemented his reputation in the film business.

In the movie, Rachel Tensions, a drag queen who sets off on a cross-country road trip, is played by RuPaul. Beyond his drag character, his performance won praise from the critics and demonstrated his acting prowess. With pioneering ideas of identity and self-acceptance, "To Wong Foo" praised drag culture.

RuPaul made cameos in television series, playing supporting characters on well-known programs including "Sabrina, the Teenage Witch" and "Walker, Texas Ranger." His performances often included aspects of drag and self-expression, and his charm and larger-than-life attitude made him a remarkable guest star.

But "The RuPaul Show," which he hosted himself, allowed RuPaul to excel as a television personality. The program lasted from 1996 to 1998 and included musical performances, celebrity interviews, and talks on a variety of subjects, such as LGBTQ+ problems and self-empowerment. "The RuPaul Show" was a trailblazing platform that championed diversity and gave the LGBTQ+ community a voice.

RuPaul's most notable and long-lasting contribution to the entertainment business, despite his success in music, film, and television, is still "RuPaul's Drag Race." He produced and hosted a reality competition program that has grown to be an international force in drag culture and LGBTQ+ visibility.

Philanthropy and Advocacy

RuPaul has devoted himself to campaigning and charity outside of his entertainment profession, utilizing his platform to promote LGBTQ+ rights and aid several philanthropic endeavors. His advocacy work has centered on eradicating prejudice and fostering self-acceptance while also bringing attention to LGBTQ+ problems.

For marriage equality and LGBTQ+ rights, RuPaul has been a vocal supporter. He joined the clamor of people and groups calling for the legal recognition of same-sex weddings by using his notoriety and power to lend his voice to the cause. In 2015, same-sex marriage became legally recognized in the United States thanks in part to his activism.

RuPaul has continually underlined the need to accept and love oneself throughout his career. Many LGBTQ+ people who have self-identity and self-worth issues have adopted his slogan, "If you can't love yourself, how in the hell are you gonna love somebody else?" as their motto. For individuals who have experienced prejudice or internalized homophobia, RuPaul's message of self-empowerment and honesty has had a powerful impact. He has exhorted people to accept who they are, to reject what society expects of them, and to take pleasure in their individuality.

HIV/AIDS awareness and prevention are included in RuPaul's advocacy efforts. He has participated in initiatives to increase knowledge of the illness and support responsible sex practices. His activities have included taking part in HIV/AIDS fundraising events and speaking out about how the disease has affected the LGBTQ+ community.

RuPaul has worked tirelessly in charity in addition to his advocacy activity. He has contributed to several philanthropic causes and organizations, such as those that help the homeless, mental health, and LGBTQ+ kids. RuPaul has improved the lives of several people and communities via her charity giving and fundraising initiatives.

RuPaul's "RuPaul's Drag Race Werq the World" tour is one of his major charitable initiatives. "RuPaul's Drag Race" queens participate throughout this world tour, which benefits charities and organizations for LGBTQ+ people. The tour provides a platform for vital issues as well as showcasing the artistry of drag queens.

RuPaul is known and respected as an advocate and philanthropist due to his dedication to giving back to the LGBTQ+ community and society at large. His charitable efforts and campaigning have matched his work in the entertainment industry, leaving a rich legacy that goes beyond his drag image.

RuPaul has received various prizes and distinctions, which have strengthened his impact on LGBTQ+ culture and rights. He was the first drag queen to get a star on the Hollywood Walk of Fame in 2018, making history in the process. The award represented a major change in society's recognition of drag as a valid and recognized art form in addition to honoring his accomplishments in the entertainment industry.

RuPaul has also received GLAAD Media Awards in recognition of his work to advance positive LGBTQ+ representation in the media. In recognition of his revolutionary influence on popular culture, he has received the MTV Trailblazer Award.

In recent years, RuPaul's work has gone beyond charity and campaigning to include education. For young LGBTQ+ people and aspiring drag queens everywhere, he has emerged as a mentor and an inspiration. RuPaul has given advice, encouragement, and priceless life lessons via his broadcast platform and public engagements.

RuPaul has had an incalculable influence on the LGBTQ+ community and society at large. His diverse career in music, cinema, television, and activism has left a lasting legacy that encourages people to be their true selves. He has challenged preconceptions, dismantled barriers, and cultivated a more welcoming and inclusive society by using his skill, charm, and influence.

His music, which is distinguished by uplifting and catchy tunes, has had a profound impact on popular culture. His journey into television hosting and acting demonstrated his flexibility and charm as a performer. But "RuPaul's Drag Race" is largely responsible for his stature as a television celebrity and for the creation of a global cultural phenomenon.

RuPaul is a strong advocate for change outside of the entertainment industry thanks to his support of LGBTQ+ rights, HIV/AIDS awareness, and self-acceptance. He has benefited people and communities via his humanitarian work and support for charity initiatives. Beyond his drag character, RuPaul has left a lasting legacy that encourages allies and LGBTQ+ people to embrace authenticity and work for a more open, accepting society.

Chapter 7: Challenges and Triumphs

Facing Adversity

Success seldom comes easy, and RuPaul Charles' career has not been an exception. A narrative of overcoming difficulties, both emotionally and professionally, lies behind the glitz, the charm, and the larger-than-life presence. In this chapter, we explore the struggles RuPaul has faced throughout his life and the tenacity that has enabled him to prevail.

Financial hardships and family difficulties characterized RuPaul's early years. RuPaul was raised in a working-class home and was born in San Diego, California, in 1960. When he was still a small child, his parents were divorced, and in his late teens, he briefly lost his house. RuPaul was driven by these early difficulties to develop a strong feeling of independence and resolve.

The obstacles of growing up in America as a young, Black, and LGBT person were unique. RuPaul's distinct personality and goals were faced with prejudice and opposition in a culture where conformity was often valued above distinctiveness. He encountered prejudice and homophobia, which spurred his determination to demonstrate that he could be successful on his terms.

RuPaul's attempt to get into the entertainment business was rejected and regarded with suspicion. He had many obstacles as a drag performer trying to break through in a field that at the time had little to no representation for them. RuPaul often heard that he didn't fit the typical model of a celebrity and that casting agencies and record companies were reluctant to support his ideas.

RuPaul was unaffected by these difficulties, however. Instead, they gave him the drive to pave his way. His experience proved that hardship may act as a motivating factor for achievement. RuPaul's perseverance and tenacity moved him ahead, and the release of "Supermodel (You Better Work)" marked his breakthrough in the music business.

Challenges, both personally and professionally

Personal and professional obstacles that challenged RuPaul's resolve came along with his rise to popularity. The death of Renetta, his younger sister, to cancer was one of his greatest challenges. RuPaul was profoundly and irreparably affected by her demise, which had a long-lasting effect on him.

RuPaul relied on his inner fortitude and the support of his close-knit family to get over this sorrow. He shared his sister's experience to encourage people to seek medical assistance when necessary by using his platform to spread awareness about cancer and the value of early diagnosis. RuPaul's capacity to use personal suffering as a platform for advocacy and emancipation is a testament to his fortitude in the face of difficulty.

RuPaul had professional difficulties as his career developed. Although "Supermodel (You Better Work)" propelled him to fame, sustaining that level of achievement was difficult. Due to the cyclical nature of the music business, RuPaul's following albums did not have the same degree of commercial success as his first.

Maintaining a long-lasting career may be challenging in the entertainment industry, as trends and preferences change quickly. RuPaul's forays into acting and television hosting have received varying degrees of praise, and not every project he has worked on has been a critical or financial success. RuPaul's capacity to adjust, change direction, and reinvent himself in the face of failures in his career, however, is evidence of his tenacity and perseverance.

RuPaul's experience with "RuPaul's Drag Race" has its share of difficulties as well. Even though the program has gained widespread acclaim, its early years were not without controversy and opposition. A drag queen-focused reality competition program was hesitantly approved by several networks and producers. The acceptance of drag culture by mainstream audiences has been questioned.

Even after the program's premiere, it took some time for "RuPaul's Drag Race" to become popular and start attracting viewers. Budget and production issues plagued the program in its early seasons, but RuPaul and his crew persisted. They had faith in the show's ability to highlight the skills and tenacity of drag queens, and their perseverance paid off.

Within the LGBTQ+ community, RuPaul also encountered opposition and controversy.

"RuPaul's Drag Race" may have fostered negative stereotypes or failed to be inclusive enough, according to certain community members. The backlash to RuPaul's remarks, particularly on trans and non-binary competitors, sparked critical discussions about representation and diversity in drag culture.

RuPaul was compelled by these obstacles to face challenging inquiries about the significance and accountability of the program. They also emphasized the need for the drag community's continuing development and conversation. RuPaul is dedicated to development and self-improvement as seen by his desire to participate in these discussions and advance his comprehension of diversity and representation.

Resilience of RuPaul

RuPaul stands out not because of the lack of difficulties but rather because of his exceptional fortitude in the face of hardship. His rise from a young, struggling performer to a recognized icon throughout the world is evidence of his unshakeable confidence in himself and his goals.

Being able to turn obstacles into opportunities is one of RuPaul's greatest assets. He has continuously utilized challenges and failures as fuel for both career and personal development. His experiences with prejudice, homelessness, and rejection inspired him to disprove his critics.

RuPaul's adaptability and capacity for self-reinvention are other examples of his tenacity. He persevered despite obstacles, whether they were financial or essential. Instead, he experimented with different fields including acting and television until finding success with "RuPaul's Drag Race." His successful career has been largely attributed to his ability to welcome change and shift course when required.

RuPaul's fortitude is seen in his advocacy efforts. He was not afraid to engage in unpleasant talks when faced with criticism or controversy. He conversed instead, took responsibility for his errors, and tried to build a more welcoming and varied drag community. He is dedicated to development and growth as seen by his readiness to change and alter his viewpoints.

RuPaul's sense of self and unshakeable honesty are also key components of his resiliency. He has never sacrificed his individuality or stayed loyal to himself throughout his career. He believes that accepting one's actual self is the key to overcoming hardship. His message of self-acceptance is captured in his catchphrase, "If you can't love yourself, how in the hell are you gonna love somebody else?"

His unwavering self-confidence also contributes to RuPaul's fortitude. Even when others questioned him, he constantly had faith in his ability and vision. His self-assurance served as the impetus that carried him to success and allowed him to encourage others to have faith in themselves.

RuPaul's capacity for adapting, evolving, and turning difficulties into victories is evidence of his everlasting confidence in himself and his mission. Along with helping him succeed, his tenacity has also allowed him to positively influence how LGBTQ+ people are seen and accepted in society. All people who experience hardship may draw inspiration from RuPaul's path, which serves as a reminder that with resiliency, honesty, and self-assurance they can overcome any challenge and realize their goals.

Chapter 8: The Man Behind the Glam

A Private Life

A name that conjures up images of glitz, charm, and out-of-this-world performances is that of the legendary drag queen and pop sensation RuPaul Charles. However, the drag superstar has carefully guarded a secret life that lurks behind the limelight and expensive personalities. We dive into RuPaul's personal life in this chapter and examine the facets of his life that are often kept out of the public eye.

RuPaul chose to retain his sense of authenticity and avoid the complications of stardom by keeping his personal life distinct from his public persona. RuPaul has always been cautious about the information he divulges, preferring to highlight his profession and the importance of self-expression while still disclosing certain facts about his personal life in interviews and autobiographies.

Relationship with Georges LeBar is one of the most well-known areas of RuPaul's private life. At the Limelight nightclub in New York City, the two first met in the early 1990s, and they hit it off right away. RuPaul's life, which was often dominated by the volatility and pressures of the show industry, benefited from Georges' sense of security and grounding as a rancher and painter.

Despite their deep affection and dedication for one another, RuPaul and Georges have decided to keep a large portion of their relationship private. They seldom ever appear together in public or divulge personal information about their relationship. Because he believes that certain elements of life should be treasured and shielded from the prying eyes of the media and the general public, RuPaul has chosen to keep this seclusion.

RuPaul's experiences with fame and the intrusive nature of the entertainment business have both had an impact on his decision to maintain a private life apart from his public image. He has seen how the media can sensationalize and use personal information, therefore he has made the decision to keep his private life out of the public eye.

RuPaul's dedication to privacy is also in line with his philosophy of honesty and self-empowerment. According to him, it is up to each person to establish their limits and select which details of their life they wish to reveal to the public. RuPaul promotes self-care and the protection of one's wellbeing by maintaining a certain measure of privacy.

Relationships of RuPaul personally

RuPaul has had several meaningful relationships throughout his life, but one of the longest-lasting and most well-known is with Georges LeBar.

RuPaul has relied on and found strength in individuals' capacity to connect deeply and meaningfully with him throughout his life.

The connection he has with his family is among the most significant ties in RuPaul's life. RuPaul still has a strong bond with his mother Ernestine Charles and his three sisters despite the difficulties he had to overcome as a child. His family has been a constant source of love and support, and they have taken great satisfaction in his accomplishments.

Another illustration of the value of being true to oneself comes from RuPaul's connection with his family. The acceptance and affection of his family have influenced his transformation from a young child with a flair for elegance to a worldwide drag legend. RuPaul has been able to be honest and follow his aspirations with confidence because of their unfailing support.

RuPaul has developed personal connections that have been essential in his life in addition to his family. He often refers to the other drag queens as his "drag family," and he has a close relationship with each of them. RuPaul has worked with other queens and performed with them throughout his career, forging bonds of sisterhood and community that go beyond the stage.

Inspiring ideas and joint projects have come from RuPaul's friendships. The queens that have participated in "RuPaul's Drag Race" have often developed into close friends and allies. Because of his generosity and dedication to fostering the drag community's elevation, RuPaul has been able to build these relationships and provide other drag queens a stage to shine on.

Being true to oneself

The significance of being true to oneself is at the heart of both RuPaul's philosophy and her public message. He has lived by this idea all of his life and throughout his career, embracing his individuality and inspiring others to do the same.

RuPaul faced difficulties along the way to honesty and self-acceptance. He experienced prejudice and homophobia as a young, Black, and homosexual person growing up in America. Nevertheless, these encounters eventually influenced his resolve to be utterly authentic.

One of the most well-known components of RuPaul's message of self-acceptance is his catchphrase, "If you can't love yourself, how in the hell are you going to love somebody else?" For those who are LGBTQ+ or are having identity issues, this simple yet meaningful remark has become a source of empowerment.

In his drag character, RuPaul displays his conviction in the virtues of self-love and self-expression. He has praised the art of metamorphosis and the opportunity to express oneself in any manner by donning glitzy and ostentatious drag outfits. RuPaul's drag character is proof that identity is malleable and can be explored and enjoyed in a variety of contexts.

RuPaul's dedication to honesty goes beyond his drag character. Whether a person is in drag or not, he exhorts them to accept who they are in all facets of their life. He has established limits to safeguard his authenticity and well-being, one of which is his choice to keep his private life private.

His advocacy work has also been inspired by RuPaul's theme of keeping true to oneself. According to him, people may question preconceptions, dismantle obstacles, and effect constructive social change by being genuine and unapologetic. The transformational power of honesty and self-love is shown by his journey from a little child with a dream to a worldwide drag celebrity.

His connections in the drag world, his relationship with Georges LeBar, and his close-knit family have all had a big impact on his life. Along the way, these relationships have given him love, support, and inspiration.

Staying loyal to oneself is the core lesson of RuPaul's philosophy. His commitment to self-acceptance, self-love, and self-expression has inspired many others to embrace their individuality and question social standards. Beyond the glitz and the stage, RuPaul's legacy serves as a reminder that authenticity is a source of power and that by being true to oneself, one can overcome difficulty and motivate others to do the same.

Chapter 9: Legacy and Influence

RuPaul's Everlasting Impact

RuPaul Charles has left behind a legacy that is nothing short of extraordinary in the fields of entertainment, LGBTQ+ activism, and self-empowerment. He became an iconic personality praised for his charm, individuality, nerve, and brilliance throughout his career, leaving an enduring impression on popular culture. In this chapter, we examine RuPaul's continuing influence and how he has changed the entertainment industry and the culture around self-acceptance.

The reality competition show "RuPaul's Drag Race," which first debuted in 2009, has become a cultural phenomenon in and of itself, and RuPaul's role as host and creator of it is one of his most important contributions to popular culture. Viewers from all around the globe have found resonance in its distinctive fusion of creativity, competitiveness, and personal narrative.

The television series "RuPaul's Drag Race" has given drag queens a stage on which to display their skills and has transformed drag from a marginalized subculture into a revered art form. The show's influence on drag culture is immense since it has helped drag performers feel a feeling of sisterhood and community. Drag further cemented its position in popular culture when contestants went on to pursue lucrative careers in music, acting, and activism.

In addition, "RuPaul's Drag Race" has been crucial for LGBTQ+ representation on television. The program is a forerunner for inclusiveness because of its diverse cast of queens, who represent a range of cultures, nationalities, and gender identities. Important dialogues regarding the intersectionality of identity and representation within the drag community have been sparked by it.

RuPaul's support of LGBTQ+ rights and self-acceptance has made a significant difference. His message of self-love and sincerity, summed up in his catchphrase "If you can't love yourself, how in the hell are you gonna love somebody else?" has inspired LGBTQ+ people and anyone who is having identity issues.

RuPaul's dedication to promoting drag talent also extends to his international spin-offs of "RuPaul's Drag Race," such as "RuPaul's Drag Race UK," "RuPaul's Drag Race Canada," and "RuPaul's Drag Race Down Under," which have introduced viewers all over the world to the rich and varied drag scenes in various nations. RuPaul's impact has spread outside of the US, demonstrating the universality of drag culture.

Motivating future generations

Beyond his influence on the entertainment business, RuPaul's legacy includes his role in empowering and inspiring younger generations. For LGBTQ+ youngsters and aspiring drag queens, RuPaul has served as a mentor, role model, and source of inspiration throughout his career.

The value of honesty and self-acceptance is one of the teachings RuPaul teaches that stick with people the longest. People from various walks of life have identified with his conviction that accepting one's genuine self is the road to empowerment. Particularly LGBTQ+ adolescents have found comfort and direction in RuPaul's message, which serves as a reminder that their identity should be cherished rather than concealed.

Aspiring queens have undergone significant change as a result of RuPaul's ability to foster a feeling of camaraderie and support among the drag community. He has given up-and-coming talent a stage to display their talents and tell their tales via "RuPaul's Drag Race." The show's participants have encouraged people to share their candid conversations on their paths to self-acceptance by doing so.

RuPaul's interactions with competitors on "RuPaul's Drag Race" are also indicative of his function as a mentor and source of advice for drag queens, and these encounters have aided contestants in developing as performers and people. The show's queen contestants often talk about RuPaul's impact and the important things they have picked up from him.

RuPaul's effect on future generations can also be observed in the drag culture that has developed as a result of "RuPaul's Drag Race," which has helped drag transform from a disregarded subculture into a revered and renowned art form. The queens that have graced the "Drag Race" stage serve as role models and sources of inspiration for upcoming drag artists.

RuPaul's support of LGBTQ+ rights and HIV/AIDS awareness has offered encouragement and direction to individuals who are impacted by these problems. Others have been motivated to follow his example by using their platforms to spread awareness and aid charity organizations. RuPaul's impact goes beyond entertainment; it is a testimony to the effectiveness of activism and awareness in bringing about constructive change.

Awards and distinctions

Throughout his career, RuPaul has received countless awards and accolades for his work in the entertainment industry, LGBTQ+ visibility, and self-acceptance. These honors are a fitting tribute to his significant influence on both popular culture and society at large.

His star on the Hollywood Walk of Fame is among the most notable awards given to RuPaul. His distinction as a pioneer in the entertainment industry was cemented in 2018 when he became the first drag queen to win this coveted award. In addition to honoring his accomplishments in the entertainment business, the celebrity also stands for a watershed point in the acknowledgment of drag as a respectable and genuine art form.

The GLAAD Media Awards honor people and media organizations for their admirable representations of LGBTQ+ people and problems in the media. RuPaul has also received one of these honors. These awards highlight his contribution to media diversity and inclusiveness and his efforts in advancing positive LGBTQ+ representation via "RuPaul's Drag Race."

Additionally, in recognition of his revolutionary influence on pop culture, RuPaul received the MTV Trailblazer Award. He has become a role model for young people seeking their paths to self-discovery and empowerment because of his capacity to defy stereotypes, push limits, and encourage self-acceptance.

RuPaul is well-known within the LGBTQ+ community as a result of his campaigning and impact. For LGBTQ+ people and their supporters, he has been hailed as an inspiration and an idol. The significant influence of his work is shown by his legacy as a pioneer for self-acceptance and representation in the community.

RuPaul's impact may also be seen in "RuPaul's Drag Race"'s ongoing success, which has been shown by the countless seasons and foreign variations of the program that have been broadcast all over the globe. RuPaul's vision and the continuing influence of his invention on the reality television industry are shown by his continued success.

RuPaul Charles' lasting influence on entertainment, LGBTQ+ activism, and self-empowerment is examined in Chapter 9 of "Legacy and Influence" as a conclusion. As the host and creator of "RuPaul's Drag Race," which popularized drag culture and altered the reality television landscape, he leaves behind a lasting legacy.

In particular, LGBTQ+ youth and aspiring drag queens, RuPaul's impact extends to the empowerment and inspiration of the next generation. People from all walks of life have found his message of honesty and self-acceptance to be inspiring, helping them to remember that accepting one's genuine self is a source of strength and inspiration.

Additionally, RuPaul has received accolades for his achievements, including a plaque on the Hollywood Walk of Fame, the MTV Trailblazer Award, and the GLAAD Media Awards. These honors honor both his pioneering work in promoting LGBTQ+ visibility and inclusiveness in the media as well as the significant influence he has had on society and popular culture.

The transforming power of honesty is shown by RuPaul's legacy as a performer, supporter, and mentor. Not only has he given Drag newfound attention, but he has also questioned assumptions and cultural standards around identity and self-expression. RuPaul has evolved into a beacon of inspiration for others looking to embrace their individuality and triumph over hardship via his path of self-acceptance and resiliency.

As RuPaul's legacy develops and grows, it serves as a poignant reminder of the long-lasting influence of trailblazers in popular culture. His capacity to effect change and motivate others shows the power of one person to make a difference by being true to themselves and utilizing their position to promote good change.

The discourse about identity, acceptance, and diversity in society has been influenced by RuPaul's work beyond entertainment and campaigning. His legacy raises issues with societal conventions and questions people's assumptions about gender, expression, and acceptance. In a society where prejudice and injustice still exist, RuPaul has contributed to the advancement of greater inclusion and understanding.

Along with his influence on LGBTQ+ portrayal, RuPaul's support for HIV/AIDS awareness and prevention has been essential in spreading the word about the pandemic. His involvement in fundraising events and campaigns helped finance research and outreach initiatives, which positively impacted the lives of individuals who were afflicted by the illness. RuPaul's commitment to this cause serves as a timely reminder that activism has the power to save lives and effect good change.

People from different backgrounds and ethnicities have found resonance with RuPaul's message of self-acceptance and love. RuPaul's motto, "If you can't love yourself, how in the hell are you gonna love somebody else?" presents a potent counter-narrative in a society that often imposes unattainable beauty standards and demands to comply. It promotes a culture of self-acceptance and self-empowerment by encouraging people to place the highest value on their health and sense of worth.

The impact of RuPaul on drag culture cannot be emphasized. He has given drag queens a platform to display their artistic ability, aptitude, and distinctive viewpoints on a larger scale. The "RuPaul's Drag Race" competitors have gone on to have amazing success, appearing in movies and television shows as well as releasing music albums. These queens have reached new heights thanks to RuPaul's mentoring and direction, and the show's reputation as a launching pad for drag talent is still strong.

Furthermore, RuPaul's influence as a mentor and friend to many drag queens goes beyond the confines of television. To all who have come into contact with him, he has provided insightful counsel, encouragement, and a feeling of community. RuPaul's ability to develop relationships and support within the drag community is shown by the feeling of sisterhood and camaraderie among drag queens.

RuPaul's legacy is still a significant symbol of advancement as the LGBTQ+ community fights for more acceptance and equal rights. The transformational power of honesty and self-acceptance is shown by his rise from a young, ambitious performer to a global drag celebrity. He has shown how people may effect good change and motivate others to follow in their footsteps by embracing their genuine selves and defying cultural norms.

RuPaul has a significant impact on the greater discussion of representation in the media and entertainment. He has broken down barriers and provided opportunities for underrepresented groups as an internationally famous openly homosexual Black drag queen. His achievement casts doubt on conventional beliefs about what is feasible in a field often dominated by cisgender, heterosexual, and mostly white characters.

Finally, RuPaul Charles has left a lasting and wide-ranging legacy. His contributions to entertainment, LGBTQ+ activism, and self-empowerment are irreplaceable. As the host and creator of "RuPaul's Drag Race," he has changed the face of reality television and brought drag culture to new levels of acceptability.

People from many areas of life, especially LGBTQ+ youth and aspiring drag queens, have been inspired by RuPaul's message of honesty, self-acceptance, and self-love. Public health initiatives have been significantly impacted by his work on HIV/AIDS awareness and prevention. It is impossible to deny his impact on drag culture, with "RuPaul's Drag Race" providing as a springboard for innumerable drag queens to pursue lucrative professions.

The legacy of RuPaul also inspires people to embrace their individuality and reject stereotypes while questioning conventional standards. His success as a Black drag queen who is openly homosexual and successful in the entertainment world opens doors for further diversity and representation.

As RuPaul's journey progresses, his legacy stands as a monument to the force of sincerity, resiliency, and self-acceptance in bringing about good change and motivating others to follow suit. His influence on popular culture and society at large serves as a reminder that people may change the world by their words, deeds, and unshakable dedication to being true to themselves. For many years to come, RuPaul's impact will reverberate, leaving a deep impression on the hearts and minds of people he has touched.

Conclusion

The famous drag queen, television personality, and LGBTQ+ activist RuPaul Andre Charles is a person whose effect has extended beyond the boundaries of activism and entertainment. He transformed from a little child with a dream to a global celebrity, leaving a lasting impression on popular culture and society as a whole. It is clear that RuPaul's legacy is one of lasting inspiration, empowerment, and change as we come to a close with our examination of his extraordinary life and career.

His dedication to sincerity and self-acceptance is the foundation of RuPaul's lasting fame. He has defended the viewpoint that accepting one's genuine self is essential to empowerment and success throughout his life and work. For LGBTQ+ people and anybody battling with self-identity, his adage, "If you can't love yourself, how in the hell are you gonna love somebody else?" has been a source of inspiration.

People of various ages and identities have found resonance in RuPaul's message of self-acceptance and self-love. RuPaul's remarks give a counter-narrative that motivates people to put their well-being and self-worth above everything else in a culture that often sets unattainable beauty standards and conformity-driven demands. His message promotes a society of self-acceptance and self-empowerment that never loses its potential to motivate new generations.

The reality competition program, which debuted in 2009, has become a cultural phenomenon in and of itself, and RuPaul's reputation is intricately linked to his work as host and creator of "RuPaul's Drag Race." Viewers from all around the globe have found resonance in its distinctive fusion of creativity, competitiveness, and personal narrative.

The television series "RuPaul's Drag Race" has given drag queens a stage on which to display their skills and has transformed drag from a marginalized subculture into a revered art form. The show's influence on drag culture is immense since it has helped drag performers feel a feeling of sisterhood and community. Drag further cemented its position in popular culture when contestants went on to pursue lucrative careers in music, acting, and activism.

Furthermore, "RuPaul's Drag Race" has been crucial in advancing LGBTQ+ visibility on television. The program is a forerunner for inclusiveness because of its diverse cast of queens, who represent a range of cultures, nationalities, and gender identities. Important dialogues regarding the intersectionality of identity and representation within the drag community have been sparked by it.

A significant part of RuPaul's lasting mythology has been his support for LGBTQ+ rights and HIV/AIDS awareness. Others have been motivated to follow his example by using their platforms to spread awareness and aid charity organizations. The devotion of RuPaul to these issues serves as a reminder of the power of advocacy to save lives and effect change for the better.

RuPaul's impact also goes beyond the world of entertainment to the wider discussion of identity, acceptance, and diversity in society. He has broken down barriers and provided opportunities for underrepresented groups as an internationally famous openly homosexual Black drag queen. His achievement casts doubt on conventional beliefs about what is feasible in a field often dominated by cisgender, heterosexual, and mostly white characters.

The transforming power of honesty is shown by RuPaul's legacy as a performer, supporter, and mentor. Not only has he given Drag newfound attention, but he has also questioned assumptions and cultural standards around identity and self-expression. RuPaul has evolved into a beacon of inspiration for others looking to embrace their individuality and triumph over hardship via his path of self-acceptance and resiliency.

Last but not least, RuPaul Andre Charles will live on in the annals of entertainment and LGBTQ+ activism as a legendary figure. His unrelenting dedication to sincerity, self-acceptance, and self-love will forever be a part of him. Future generations, especially LGBTQ+ kids and aspiring drag queens, look to RuPaul as a source of inspiration and strength, and this effect extends to them.

The development of RuPaul from a young, aspiring performer to a worldwide drag celebrity shows the transforming potential of accepting one's real self and defying social norms. His influence on popular culture and society at large serves as a reminder that people may change the world by their words, deeds, and unshakable dedication to being true to themselves. All individuals who have had the honor of being impacted by RuPaul's message of love and honesty may find solace, empowerment, and change in his unwavering legacy.

Printed in Great Britain
by Amazon

34478579R00066